Praise for YO

"A compelling invitation to self discovery and the personal magic within us all. Yoram has created a book that inspires page-turning wonder as the reader discovers how natural it is to live a magical and purposeful life. The love comes through the pages....enjoy!"

—**Carl Bendix,** CEO of Jupiter Ambrosia, Architect of Change, executive producer of Maria Shriver's *The Women's Conference.*

"With his poetry, Yoram Weis offers a precious opportunity to pause from our daily fast moving pace, allowing us to rest our body and mind, and delve into "the great mystery" that is so easily taken for granted or forgotten. In this troubled world, in which so many of us live blindly as if we were immortal, these poems remind us that what is immortal is only the mysterious nature of our brief existence within the eternal cycle of life. The melodic words seem to rise into the air as if each phrase was created to inspire awareness and soothe the reader into a meditative state."

—**Idanna Pucci,** writer-filmmaker, author of *The Epic of Life* and *Against All Odds,* co-producer of *Archaeology of a Woman.*

"From the first page to the last, *You Are Your Purpose* grabs the heart and won't let go. A poetic journey into the love and wisdom of the soul, this is a beautifully written, inspirational book that awakens our deepest longings and empowers our highest dreams."

—**Prill Boyle**, author of *Defying Gravity.*

"You have no choice but to dive deep into your most gentle imagination when reading this book. Your mind opens, your heart opens, your soul opens to receive such beautiful and insightful thoughts."

—**Rachel P. Goldstein**, founder and CEO of Agent of Change.

"*You Are Your Purpose* is not your ordinary book of wispy spiritual poetry. Yoram has a poetic voice that's both muscular and tender, both simple and subtle. His words call out to a deep place in you that already knows they are true, but longs to hear them said. I felt nourished, understood, and embraced."

—**Erika Andersen**, founder of Proteus International, author of *Be Bad First* and *Leading So People Will Follow*.

"Yoram's poems return to me as a friend, reminding me of this marvelous life we share, and are embedded with the knowing of deep rivers of love. Yoram is a contemporary Kahlil Gibran, evoking universal wisdom, kindness and assurance—be yourself, know yourself, and all is well. Keeping his words close makes life's passages all the more alluring and graceful. I am ever grateful for his craft of inspiring a purposeful life, one that buoys my heart and soothes my soul."

—**Tucker Robbins**, founder and CEO of Tucker Robbins, pioneer designer and eco-socio entrepreneur.

"Yoram Weis' poetic book perfectly balances insight, depth, and soaring grace. In its pages I found phrases and imagery that nourished me like a bowl of hot soup on a cold afternoon. Dig in for a wonderful meal of sustaining inspiration."

—**Joanne Heyman**, founder and CEO of Heyman Partners.

"Yoram's eloquent authenticity and insightful reflections are deeply moving, and touch the heart with the mystical wisdom that navigates the many facets of the human experience. *You Are Your Purpose* is medicine for the soul—a truly inspirational piece of work, and an empowering journey into the beauty and magic of our soul's purpose."

—**Deborah Mills**, director of Soul Focused Healing.

"My heart was moved by these magical words. *You Are Your Purpose* is a poetic mirror to the wise and loving nature of our human purpose, a deep expression of a heart that is truly inspired. Yoram's insightful writing with its empowering spirit inspires courage and passion to pursue one's greater vision and purpose."

—**Raymond E. Belcher**, writer and director of
For Your Entertainment Pty (Australia).

"All poetry is meant to touch, move and inspire the reader. *You Are Your Purpose* excels in doing this, with an enlightened soul wisdom that Yoram culls from his own ongoing spiritual, emotional, and cognitive explorations. The title of the book doesn't do justice to his skill at guiding the heart through beautiful metaphors and soothing affirmation of all that is good and uplifting. *You Are Your Purpose* has the potential to facilitate a deep healing journey toward growth and fulfillment."

—**Linda Powers Leviton**, MA, LMFT, director of the West Coast Gifted Development Center, author of *Peace Within, Peace Between*.

"Yoram's richly lyrical prose lends wings to your heart's unspoken truth. His words of wisdom awaken your spirit and touch your soul with a gentle guidance for love and healing."

—**Helen Allen**, founder of Energising Your Life (UK).

"*You Are Your Purpose* takes the reader on a journey of deep self-discovery in a unique format of beautiful poetic passages. With each chapter building upon the last, Yoram provides insight into life's lessons and challenges, and encouragement to cherish its intimate experiences. This book is a close companion, and I highly recommend it to anyone who is seeking inspirational guidance to gain a greater understanding of their purpose on the planet."

—**Pamela Miles**, Life Midwife, founder of Wisdom of Within.

YOU ARE YOUR
PURPOSE

YOU ARE YOUR PURPOSE

Awaken Your Inner Magic, Self-Love, and Clarity of Purpose

YORAM WEIS

INWARD PORTAL PRESS
Asheville, North Carolina

You Are Your Purpose: Awaken Your Inner Magic, Self-Love, and
Clarity of Purpose / Yoram Weis

Published in the United States of America by:

Inward Portal Press
Asheville, North Carolina

First edition, January 2016

Edited by: Marilyn Jayne Owen
Cover and interior design by: Emma Grace

Images credits:
Cover image: Neo Edmund / Shutterstock
Mandala design: by Freepik
Image page xiv: Fona / Shutterstock
Image page 204: Zuzana Dolinay / Shutterstock

Library of Congress Control Number: 2015919440

Inward Portal Press, Asheville NC

ISBN: 978-0-9970499-0-9
ISBN-10: 0-9970499-0-1

Printed in the United States of America

I dedicate this book to you, Sophia, the love of my life.
You are a well of soul wisdom, my angel of beauty and joy,
and I love you so dearly.
You have been a lucid star of hope in my darker hours,
and a wise mirror to my heart, as we soar in our light,
in the ever-expanding expressions of our souls.

And to my beloved parents, Rachel and Jochai, thank you for
being such amazing human beings and nurturing parents.
I love you and am forever grateful for the depth of your
love and wisdom, and for sharing so much of
our souls with each other on this journey.

Contents

Let no fear mask the beauty of your inner calling,
no doubt deflate the buoyancy of your purpose.
Stand tall in the nature of your soul.
With this body you shall walk the earth,
but with your heart you shall walk the sky.

—YW

Preface

What starts in your heart as a whisper can grow to a thunder of change in the world.

What defines the inner whisper is not its subtle voice, but the way it calls us into the wisdom of our soul. There, in the stillness that precedes words and thoughts, we listen to the secrets of life, the way a tree would listen to the roots that nurture its dreams. In that inner space, we are summoned to embrace our deepest nature, draw on our true strength and courage, and awaken to our authentic gifts and magic.

At our roots, we are conscious beings propelled through life by a deep quest and a unique personal calling. We rise like a wave from the deep realm of our soul, and never really detach from the body of love upon which we travel in pursuit of our purpose. We are always a part of this boundless ocean of existence, and in all phases of our life we are forever its expression of passion and creativity.

This world is an amplifier of experiences and life lessons. The whisper in our heart leads us like an intuitive wind through the uncertainty of this world, drawing us nearer to who we really are.

If we let it, it will guide us into the adventures we were born to experience. Our path is personal and unique. It is when we lean into each moment of life, and fearlessly live what we love, that our whisper turns into thunder. Empowered in our authentic purpose, embodying our gifts and lessons, humbled by and grateful for our transformation, we become attuned to Life's deepest music.

I created this book for you as an expression of what I have witnessed in my life, within and without. We are like travelers who gather around the campfire of hearts to tell our stories, sing our songs, and share our souls, in gratitude for life's magic. I share my experience in the poetic language of the heart, the most ancient and innovative tongue—the voice of the soul, where feelings and thoughts are cuddled by the silence of our deep knowing.

The eleven chapters of the book take you through a life journey, inspired by a persistent inner calling, through the different phases of its transformation and growth. Catalyzed by the inner magic of our boundless nature, we journey from the threshold of thirst, through the cycles of our life lessons, the uncovering of innate gifts, and the emerging of our inner wisdom. In this courageous quest, we face some challenges that drive us into the inner shadows of our subconscious realms, where we find new treasures and rise again with a wider view of life and deeper authenticity. We meet our subtle intuitive side, and connect with the resources, knowledge, and creativity of our higher nature. We venture the infinite fields of love, through the transforming power of relationships, and the nurturing beauty of self-love.

Empowered by the wisdom we have gained and the limitations we have shed, we spread our creative wings of vision. What had first to sprout in our heart, mature in our life, and be owned by our free will, can now blossom to a wider creative expression. Our life purpose evolves through the sculpting and refining of our own character and values, as we grow into our personal calling. In time, we will roll like thunder in the expression of our heart, always preceded by the lightning of our own inner change.

This inner change, integrated into the way we show up, and the awareness we exercise in engaging life, all translate to our generous contribution to the change in the world. Like thunder, our voices and our actions carry the aroma of the coming rain, the nourishing abundance of evolution, as it pushes existence beyond its boundaries, into its unlimited creative possibilities.

My hope is that you'll find this book an inspiring and nurturing companion on your personal journey of discovery. You can read it from start to end, gathering from its fields whatever calls to your heart. You can also spontaneously open this book at any of its pages, and allow its poetic mirrors to kindle your spirit into your own precious song.

There is no greater truth than the one unfolding from your own authentic nature and exploration. Your innate insights are all fully yours, unveiling from the depth of your own knowing, as they join the myriad of stories recounted around this campfire. My wish is to encourage and inspire you to deeply connect with your inner whisper, and be all that you are—the giant hand that tears its glove from within, with the creativity and passion of your own wisdom, love, purpose and vision.

Wherever you are on your journey, be the pioneer of your own calling. The compass in your soul is your true inner guide. The wings of your heart are your highest inspiration, and the innate compassion deep in your being is your most intimate lover. Let nothing in this world dim your light or rattle your enthusiasm. Walk your own steps, as no path would better express your purpose than being fully and truly who you are. I trust this book will echo this as you visit any of its pages, and I know your own life will echo it through every page you turn on the precious journey of your purpose.

CHAPTER 1

The Invincible Magic of You

The magic that cycles with the stars
glows also in your breath.
It rhymes with serendipity in your steps,
and unveils like grace through your choices.
It is destiny awakened by your will,
the North Star of your inner knowing.

THE CREATIVE DANCE OF PURPOSE

We are evolving artists of life,
imaginative and visionary;
magicians who are yet to master
the wands of our true calling.
Enchanted by the surging music
of our boundless dreams,
we whirl our passion into life
in the arms of the invisible.

We can hear the whisper of our heart
standing witness to our dance,
breathing like silence in our longing,
floating like a promise in our trance,
awaking threads of deeper knowing,
as we shed away our old beliefs.

We are human bridges from fear to love,
a distance we must cross in our heart.
We are here to assert soulful choices,
create destinies of clarity
between a restless earth and listening stars.

We are here to learn fateful lessons
that will become gifts of wisdom
in the growing sky of our compassion.

Since forever, we have been
the ebb and flow of matter and spirit,
tender fingers of awareness
caressing the skin of the divine;
vessels of magic, instruments of love –
love that transforms and refines our being,
even as we struggle to find our voices
and free our treasures into the light.

Our purpose is not as much in doing
as it is in our becoming.
We embody what we know,
and as eager seeds of life,
we must grow into this knowing.
What needs to be done
through our presence on this earth
can only unfold
through the maturity of our souls.

HOPE IS VISIONARY

Hope is more than wishful thinking –
the space you give to your higher heart,
your commitment to rise with trust,
even from the hollow of your darkest night.

It is the subtle knowledge
that you are loved beyond belief,
and that the universe is forever
invested in your growth.
The instinctive certitude
that while you cannot control
the shape of events to come,
you will prevail in your purpose,
remain authentic in your love
and true to your higher nature.

Hope is not imaginary.
It is visionary.
It glows with wisdom from your soul,
and rains compassion in your heart,
nurturing options that else
you would never dare to choose.

Hope is freedom –
weightless and infinitely graceful,
it will release you from the illusion
of what appears to your eyes
and is confined to your beliefs.
It will set you free and open
in the sky of unyielding magic,
wherein await surprising choices
that only hearts can ever see.

YOU ARE MAGIC

Magic is like a treasure box –
you find it in the deep.
Its lock eludes your logic
until you realize it needs no key.
And then, once opened,
you find your own self in it,
curled like a pearl
in the embrace of your heart.

The magic that cycles with the stars
lives also in your breath.
It speaks the language of the soul
and dances to the music of love.
It rhymes with serendipity in your steps,
and unveils like grace through your choices.
It is destiny awakened by your will,
the North Star of your inner knowing.

Engage now your deeper nature.
Weave it with authenticity
into the fabric of your daily life.

See the miracle of the ordinary –
the way your choices converge to love,
lessons leading to your higher heart.

How do we awake?
In the million ways that flowers bloom,
each by the nature of their encoding,
each by the evolution of their calling.

There are endless stars in outer space,
yet you find the truest glow within.

IN THE HEART OF LIFE

Like spirited rays from stars afar,
we leap from the infinity of light
into this unsettled world of strife
in quest of the horizons of love.
You may feel alone, exiled from home,
but you are always in the heart of life.
This thirsty journey of human passion
is not confined to its appearance –
etching our lives on the skin of earth,
we weave a world of higher nature
through the ripening of our souls.

You are not here to be tested or judged,
but to love in earnest and be loved.
To stand by your human learning,
and believe in your deepest dreams.
Vulnerable to fate, yet free in will,
you'll find compassion in your wounds,
lessons in your triumphs and failings,
new gates of insight in your daring.

In tender fields of honest sharing,
we meet ourselves in each other's hearts,
find strength in our collective wisdom,
and wider truth in each other's paths.
Let the veils of this illusion
give way to bolder, higher knowing.
The invincible magic that you own
echoes the divinity of your source.
While hidden in the density of earth,
it is evident in your lucid nature.

You are unique and truly special,
a miracle in the making.
Like a sudden rainstorm in the desert,
gathering strength from unknown sources,
you surface with your deepest gifts
and leave a blossom in your wake.

Let no fear mask
the beauty of your inner calling,
no doubt deflate
the buoyancy of your purpose.
Stand tall in the nature of your soul.
With this body you shall walk the earth,
but with your heart, you shall walk the sky.

Fuller than the Moon

How often you whisper in my heart
the intoxicating secrets of love.
How deeply you enter my longing
through the sweetness of our silence.

Since forever, you are present in my breath,
intimate like passion on the lips of love.
Your inner gaze, fuller than the moon,
inspires the fullness of my being.

There is no warmer touch
than that of your tender kindness.
Often you have caressed my heart
with the softness of your love.

I meet you in my stillness
in the fields behind my thoughts.
You embrace me from within
to my infinite space of beauty.

The fragrance of your magic
is enchanting beneath my skin.
I am buoyant in your love
and my veils are growing thin.

Free and luminous in my awareness,
you inspire wisdom of higher realms.
You breathe courage in my sails
and fervor beneath my wings.

You, my beloved higher nature,
are everything I am yet to learn.
You are home to my expanding heart,
my essence, whispering my dreams.

How precious it is to be awakened
by your call within my soul.
I let go to your boundless magic,
falling deeper in your embrace
to rise higher in my love.

LUCID DREAM

Enter this dream world lightly,
like a whisper from realms of silence.
Journey the earth with weightless heart,
like a scent of love from inner blossom.

Nothing here is the way it seems –
more than a story is being told,
and most of it remains invisible.
When you are aware you are dreaming,
seek the presence of the dreamer.
Find the true thread in your quest,
the one that, even in your dream,
calls for your awakening.

Too subtle is your essence
to become a part of this world,
too free is your soul
to be caged in your mind.
Visit this world like you visit a dream –
come and go in the middle of a song,
and let your soul guide your singing.

Be of the nature of your light –
glow in the darkness, not to repel,
but to embrace everything in you
that yearns to be seen by your love.

Rise on the horizons of each day
to see behind the faces of life
that which is faceless and formless.
Then set into your inner world
to leave all you have learnt behind,
your lessons ripened in the fields,
where you have danced your ego
into wings.

Enter gently and leave gracefully.
Caress this existence with kindness,
so it may refine your thirsty spirit.
Live in freedom, like a lover of life,
present in the listening of your soul.
Do not drown in this elusive ocean,
surf its waves like a breath of life.
However far you sail in this dream,
awake within it buoyant with love.

THE PHOENIX OF LOVE

The phoenix rises not only from ashes,
but also from its deeply rooted fears.
It rises from the doubts burning its body
and from the wounds salting its tears.

What are fears but the long shadows
of your towering, purest love?
Bound to your light, they feed only
on your choice to give them life.

Face your light like a planet
mirroring its star,
and grow taller in your purpose.
Spread wider and braver wings
to defy the gravity of doubts,
and reach to touch the higher sky
with your gifts and thirsty visions.

Magic is your deeper nature,
made visible through your wakeful love;
the subtle home, where you are nurtured
by the clarity of your inner work
and the freedom of your self-belief.

Work first on what you truly care for,
and trust the wisdom in your heart.
Share what you really mean to say,
and stand for your widest view of life.
The virtue you live by is what you become.

You will always be greater than your fears.
Your feet are small, but they'll walk the length
of the land you are set to cross.
Your giant spirit moves not by force,
but by the power that moves your breath.
In time you will see it all
with eyes of love and grateful heart,
so let your burden vanish now
and let it find its resting place.

Rise fearlessly to your newborn sky,
where your memories cannot fly,
and old beliefs can only die;
where new beginnings soar to magic,
like a phoenix that has faced its fears,
and, in seeing them, rose to love.

MULTIDIMENSIONAL JOURNEY

We float on the surface of existence,
boats of dreams in waves of uncertainty.
Our sails hang high in the winds of change,
our gaze pries the horizons
in search of a shore we could call our home.

But our true purpose resides in the deep.
It lies beneath and above us,
within and all around our presence.
It is in the abundance of the ocean
that keeps us afloat,
and in every breath weaving us to life.
It is in the currents that steer us
across the veils of mystery,
and in the intimate stillness
concealing the secrets of our soul.
It is never absent,
its whisper never far from our heart,
its wings awaiting our choices.

We are multidimensional beings
in a boundless breathing creation.

From the subtle realms of our souls
to our grounded presence here,
we are only separated inside our minds.
Our true nature is infinite oneness,
from which all life extends like waves,
moving in their connective dance
across the surface of perception.
We are of passion and of stardust,
here to explore the nature of love,
scattered into fragments of awareness
like sensors in countless human bodies.

Infinite are the human choices,
and our destiny is an open quest.
Yet our essence is fully present
in all the windows of our hearts,
our thirst is charged with purpose,
embedded with our deepest trust.

To be opened up like eyelids
on the timeless face of love,
melt like a tear of faith
into mighty rivers of compassion,
on our daring passage of becoming.

CHAPTER 2

In the Window of Longing

How precious and unforgettable
are the sweet lips of life
that meet your prayers with a kiss
at each turn of this journey,
lending silence to your longing
in the kind embrace of trust.

IF YOU CAN HEAR YOUR HEART

If you can hear your heart,
give it the space of your dreams.
Open wide your windows to the sky,
and light it up with your passion.

Leave no shadow unexplored,
no vision unimagined,
no longing unheeded,
and no silence unloved.

This thirst in your heart
is the rising wave of who you are.
Yearning for the shores of awareness,
it has the whole ocean behind it,
forever exhaling into life
every sound, fragrance and color
of your deepest gifts.

If you can hear your soul's whisper,
know it has already heard your prayers.
Like an eager wind it has gathered

each echo of your longing,
and from afar it has drawn in
all the fragments of your love.

Watch it now, bursting open
each cage in your cluttered mind,
freeing birds of elated visions,
hidden in your higher nature.

Trust the instinct of your calling,
and with freedom in your heart,
boldly step into your light.

THE SEED OF DESTINY

Our nature is like a seed
floating in the wind.
Seemingly lost, it will
journey for great distances
before it lands on its purpose.

But when it does,
it sprouts and blossoms
with such vigor and passion,
it will transform any landscape
into forests of abundance.

Destiny is purpose made visible,
longing heeded by your will,
a deep vision born to life
from an ancient promise in your soul.

A promise you now embrace
as your sweet awakening
at the tail end of this dream.
A new beginning already knocks
from within the doors of your heart.

There is no seed that does not carry
a tree or a flower in its womb.
In your dreams you may imagine castles,
but when the seed of your true nature
sinks its roots in your awareness,
life itself becomes your garden.

Its fragrance will fill your air
with the oxygen of love –
love that will melt your thirst to water,
and lay your quest to rest
in the silent work of your soul.

LEARN TO FLY

Your wings are the part of your heart,
uncontainable by your body.
Where they long to fly is
both your home and your destiny.
They do not belong to this world,
and are forever free within it.

They cannot control the winds of fate,
yet their flight is attuned to your calling.
Their passion is weightless,
and their strength is your will.
Often you have touched the sky,
riding their buoyant fervor,
forever expanding your views.

They fly like music, surging with joy,
inspired by your instinct of purpose.
They toss your stories to the wind,
like leaves of fading seasons
from the forests in your mind,
writing your destiny in the sky
with choices of higher wisdom.

Your wings extend from your heart,
and carry the cellular memory
of your inherent freedom.
Not until you learn to love yourself
with the same passion that makes them fly,
will you soar to the true heights
of your being.

This is not only your life's deepest lesson –
this is the nature of authentic living.

MY DOOR IS WIDE OPEN

My door is wide open.
I have no walls standing.
My thirst has emptied the horizons,
leaving only self-love
to gaze back at my tears.

There is no ceiling to my longing
and no locks on my heart.
I have heard the whisper of life
from within my breath,
and held its beloved face
in the palms of my prayers.

There are no road signs
on my path ahead.
It lies before me
like a field of mystery,
flooded by my passion
in search of my boat.

I do have my trusted sails.
They are tall, and fortified

by years of surrender to the winds.
Their wounds were sewn up by
the gentle needles of forgiveness,
and their fabric made transparent
by the salt of humbling seas.

My mouth is now speechless.
It has turned its voice over
to my wiser heart.
My spirit has journeyed into the mist,
and returned silent but elated,
carrying in its feathers
the scent of new beginnings.

In its silence,
a message echoes from within:
There are no endings for lovers,
and no walls in their dwellings.
There are only wings of trust
to the body of my longing,
gathering strength and courage,
as they listen to and soar with
the eternal calling of my soul.

LIVING IT LIKE WAVES

To be so perfectly imperfect,
so timely, yet out of sync.
To be so repeatedly clueless,
and yet, so authentic
in our longing for love,
so relentless in our efforts
to live by its beauty.

Our longing is a human journey
across an ocean of uncertainty,
whose mystery is vowed to silence.
We live it like waves of hope,
exhaled from the heart of compassion,
rising from stillness to awareness,
one breath at a time.

No matter how many times
the shores of this world will reject us,
our nature will keep rising from the deep,
and we shall set forth once again
with a passion that will never rest
away from love.

Such is the longing in our soul,
that it will embrace
the whole time and space
from within,
until our dreams mature to wisdom,
and our hearts turn ageless in love.

What we live as waves
we breathe as an ocean,
and from deep within,
embrace it into the stillness
of who we truly are.

COME CLOSER STILL

Come closer still.
I have no skin left
to separate me
from what I am in you.
My breath
has melted in your love,
and it flows like water into air,
soaring like silence into light.

I am a dream within your heart,
and all I can dream of
is your boundless presence,
ever still,
buoyant with kindness,
embracing my thirsty space
like a long awaited lover
from within.

Come closer still.
Let no veils lie to me
about distances of time
and gaps between the worlds.

I would patiently wait for you
if I could,
but it is you, not me,
who does the waiting.

Come, sit in,
rest within my heart,
where not even silence
can conceal you.
Let me plunge into your beauty
in the lucid wells of my longing,
dive as deep as stillness goes,
until you breathe me softly,
from within,
into the silky space of love.

THE MIST OF LONGING

The mist of longing rises slowly
over the bay of my heart.
The soft distant sounds
of valleys abandoned by fate,
of cities forsaken by dreams,
drift away, as if stolen
by the silence in my soul.

My heart speaks without words,
and its anxious, restless winds
blow unchecked in my windows.
I am bound by cords of memories,
mystified by what has been lost,
too weary to cross the ocean ahead.

Ever deep is the closure of destiny,
and too far are the new horizons.
My prayers sink like wounded boats,
and I can see nothing ahead,
as if the earth I stood upon
has been erased into space.

Love has undressed her body
to the bareness of my longing.
In this deserted hour of thirst,
humility has become my breath.
Let this emptiness in my heart
be the house where I surrender,
where I can lay my grief to rest,
let go of the world I have known,
and embrace a new world,
yet to be born.

The long corridors of forgiveness,
and the tall hallways of self-love,
must lead to doors of new beginnings.
Even now, in the mist of the nightfall,
I know that my longing is a key –
one that will unlock new treasure chests,
unveiling ever so sweetly within,
awaking like a timid new dawn
of a promise growing in my soul.

INTO YOUR WIDER NATURE

Your soul passion moves through life
like a creative force
through a field of dreams.
It paves a path of choices,
from the yearning in your breath
to the horizons of your destiny.

Like a lover, it needs to be held
in the arms of stillness,
just long enough
to mature in your heart,
to grow wings of freedom
from the body of your wisdom.

How precious and unforgettable
are the sweet lips of life
that meet your prayers with a kiss
at each turn of this journey,
lending silence to your longing
in the kind embrace of trust.

Go, burst out of the bubble
of your old limited self
to a space of no regrets and doubts,
with no memories to indulge in,
and no expectations to fulfill.

Break free and rise to your fullness
that even now glows in your sky,
where you meet your wider nature,
and give birth from your passion
to your unwavering love for life.

CHAPTER 3

The Spiral of Life Lessons

*Our soul gifts are deep treasures
drawn to surface by the whirlpools
of our inherent life lessons.
Their play is the mystical dance
between destiny and choices,
the unveiling of who we are
into a life of creative purpose.*

New Beginnings

Every phase is a new beginning,
and in every beginning
there is a new you.
Like the seasons, the cycles of life
are inherently set on nurturing growth.

Let the new you be inspired
by new visions in your heart,
not weighed down by old beliefs.
Let it be empowered by self-love,
not depleted by regrets and doubts.

Trust the strength of your soul nature –
unchangeable it moves on with you,
encoded with your life purpose,
into the new grounds you now explore
through your inner transformation.

Honor each step in your journey
with your undivided presence.
Listen deeply, even in your uncertainty,

be guided by your inner wisdom,
to see it all with newborn eyes.

Your authenticity is your gate
to infinite clarity ahead.
Even in your darkest nights,
your path of light is woven from
the luminous threads in your heart.

Glow with this inner light –
Grow tenderly from within
like the unfolding of a flower,
the emerging of a new star
in the eternal cycles of your soul..

STAIRWAY OF CHALLENGES

There is deep compassion in knowing
that the obstacles you face
are the steps you climb
to greater love and understanding.

Climb each step mindfully,
open like the listening silence,
to receive the gifts of your heart,
instead of conquering
more summits in your quest.

Let the spiral of your life lessons
be the stairway to your higher self,
and the journeys to your shadows
be the healing work of your soul.

There is no shame in your pain,
and no loss in a well learned lesson.
Life cares not how you may appear,
it grows fearlessly from your inside out,
as does the wisdom of your soul.

Do not fear the challenges
that are the catalysts of your growth,
nor block away the changes
that will free you from your doubts.
The spiral of your learning
is the refining of your spirit,
each curve away from your reluctance
is a deeper step into your truth.

Destiny is a stream of lucid dreams.
Move through them with full awareness.
Be authentic in your choices,
so each phase you wake up from
will find you in your deeper truth,
at the horizons of who you are –
upon the infinitely thin line
where your soul meets the earth.

Each sunset of your old self
is the sunrise of your fuller being.

Soul Gifts in the Making

Our soul gifts are deep treasures
drawn to surface by the whirlpools
of our inherent life lessons.
Their play is the mystical dance
between destiny and choices,
the unveiling of who we are
into a life of creative purpose.

You are not here to prove your merit,
and your path is open like arms of love.
You are a pioneer at your edge,
explorer of the nature of the soul.
Your passage to the heart of life
is a quest for a deeper view within,
witnessed between the two mirrors
of the unfolding journey of your life,
and the silent telling in your heart.

Your story shape shifts like a movie
that you still edit through your choices.
Each time you step into a moment,

you become the breath of awe,
waiting to be taken,
the presence of awaking beauty,
longing to be loved.

In the shadows beneath your thoughts,
seeds of light are in the making –
seeds you faithfully nurture
to the full blossom of your gifts.
Among the finest of your treasures
is the miracle of compassion,
your capacity for kindest love –
love of self and love for others,
as you forever expand your circle
to include all life in your greater self.

Embrace with deep respect
both the visible and invisible
dimensions of your existence.
Your virtues may be seeded on earth,
but they blossom to gardens in your spirit,
where your soul lessons become timeless,
embedded like gems of wisdom
in the eternal oneness of all love.

A WEIGHTLESS HEART

To your inspired heart,
magic is not a mystery.
Do not let the walls in your mind
define the forest you grow in.
Make space for wild flowers
in your tidy gardens,
and for birds of freedom
in your thirsty sky.

When the calling in your heart
rises to caress your wings,
it is time to become
weightless among the stars.
It is time to open wide
the gifts of your soul,
and set them free in the winds
to shine their presence in your world.

Your inspired heart is a giant
born of wonder and curiosity,
a student of the mystery of life,
an alchemist of the shadow and the light.

Fearless and eager to learn,
it will stretch you from certainty to doubt
gathering your lessons in its wings.

Ever kind in its giving,
and abundant in its sharing,
your heart will lift you to the space
of true nobility in your nature.
Keen with its creative passion,
it will spark you into brilliance,
yet wise in its detachment
it will forever guide you,
through the corridors of humility,
to the timeless patience of existence –
barefoot on the path of love.

Set Sail

The cycles of fate
are also cycles of wisdom,
a relentless spiral of learning,
triggered by your deepest passion.
You navigate the waves of change
with the courage of your choices,
embracing each life lesson
into the heart of your transformation.

Unstoppable are the cycles of your life,
so let all your worries fall away
from the windows of your mind.
See clearly, not only your intentions,
but the guidance deep in your heart,
the seeds of destiny only you can grow,
and the visions hidden in your prayers.

Do your listening within your breath,
in the deep stillness that is
everywhere without moving,
and everything without owning.

The winds of changes will stir your ocean,
but your knowing is stirred by your soul.

Set sail for the voyage of seers.
Accept no doubt on your journey,
and no regrets in its wake.
Leave behind your outdated charts –
where you go is not yet on a map,
and will emerge only by your seeing.

Let your soul steer your course,
and skip no lesson on your way,
so what belongs to you
may meet you on your path,
and the promise of your birth
become the composer of your life.

Do not stop at the known horizons
when your journey takes you to the stars.
There are no walls to your house of learning,
your freedom is a ceaseless wheel train
in the eternal movement of your soul.

THE EYE OF THE STORM

Your life lessons whirl around your purpose
like a storm around its core of stillness.
Each ending longs for a new beginning,
each cycle reaches for deeper learning.

The mighty forces of evolution,
summoned to refine your spirit,
will not be deterred by your defiance,
nor change their persistent nature
to appease your doubts.

In your towering clouds of emotions
there's a hidden beacon of clarity,
pulsating like passion in the mist,
beckoning you with a promise
that your soul whispers in the wind.

Your life lessons whirl around your purpose,
stirring chaos in structures of your mind,
uprooting disempowered beliefs,
freeing your love from cages of fears.

Each time, at the heart of the storm,
there rests a silence of unfettered beauty,
calling you back to the eye of your soul,
where in the blue sky of purpose,
all your lessons can be embraced,
your struggles can be honored,
and your intentions can be blessed.

We find home in the eye of the storm,
with each soul lesson we grow to own,
where chaos surrenders to stillness,
our insecurities mature to trust,
and our fears transform to self-love.

THE MIRROR OF YOUR SOUL

There are thousands of mirrors
in the river of life –
faces of people, lessons and events,
all woven in this passionate dance ,
choreographed with the wisdom
of a script deep in your soul.

Among all these reflections
is the silent mirror within,
where you see not the faces you wear,
but the observer you truly are;
not your struggles nor your lessons,
but your timeless, formless nature.

The intimate mirror of your soul
is neither veiled nor hidden.
Made transparent by your inner light,
it faces the inside,
and must be seen by your open heart.
Like an ageless witness,
it holds in its space all that was;
like a womb – all you can mature to be.

There are shadows you carry
in this unsettled river of life,
where you have buried your grief,
and have hidden your gifts.

The passage from each older self
deeper into the essence of your soul,
is the fading of your fears and doubts
in the presence of the light you are –
the transparent sweetness of your light,
embraced by the thirst in our heart.

The river of life is a surge of love.
It runs like a vein in a body of wisdom.
Each moment, each turn, is your art –
sculpting from your deepest lessons
your masterpiece of existence.

Choose wisely,
as love unveils through your choosing.
In its might it seeks not your obedience,
but the beauty of your free will.
Let your life journey be
the inspired trail you leave behind
as you move deeper into your soul.

THE ALTITUDE OF SURRENDER

Surrender is the way we move forward
when all the roads fade to nothing,
and our efforts land like tired birds
in the thirsty fields of our dreams.

We surrender –
when our deepest prayers are silenced
by the intensity of our own longing,
and our heart empties out the pages
in the withered book of destiny
that we now must author from our soul.

Surrender is never the ending,
but the return to the grand beginning,
back to the eternal mystery
of the formless realm of potential,
where possibilities wait to take form.

It is with great courage
that we find this inner strength,
and with deep humility
that we rise to the heights of such freedom.

Here, we choose not another path,
but the view from our higher heart.

From here we carve our new way
with eager steps of authenticity,
and we move like fertile silence
through the creative space of grace,
where the deepest work is truly done.

In surrendering to our essence,
the essential can now be completed.

CHAPTER 4

Your Soul's Eye View

*Lean into each experience,
each moment in your journey,
as if they were intimate doorways
to your innermost treasures.
On the path to the heart of life,
let your heart do the walking.*

Purpose Whisperer

If you keep hitting a wall,
it is simply not your door.
Walls do talk,
more often than we listen.

Our dialogue with life
is a dance of discernment.
Its music may elude us,
but our instinct is the beat.

Do not override the obvious
when it stares you in the face.
Know when it's time to let go
and seek what is yours to embrace.

Walls will unveil as your mirrors,
mountains as your stepping-stones.
On the horizon of your thirst,
your destiny will reveal the rising
of your finest portrait of love,
painted by the artist in your heart.

See always with the eyes of your soul.
Deep within,
you are your own purpose whisperer.
Choose wisely –
your real love is seeded
in your authentic knowing.
Your personal North Star
is high in your inner sky.
Its glow
has already caught your eye.

Never ever quit your heart.

Rain Love

When your heart and thoughts turn cloudy,
rain love.
To rise above your fears and self-doubts,
and break free from your fog of regrets,
is to invest in the authenticity
of your innermost nature.

The fragments of illusion
dominating your emotions
will only linger to the distance
of your own disempowerment.
Unheeded they will fade away
as you reclaim your certainty,
embracing your presence in love.

Your core passion, driving you
so deeply from within,
and your self-love, freeing
the buoyancy of your soul,
are not products of this world.
They are gifts of your nature,

endowed to you by
the wisdom of evolution.

Do not hold back your nature,
and let no cloud hide your gifts.
Rain your love in abundance,
as it is love that weaves your destiny
from its intimate threads in your heart,
each time you embrace your transformation,
each time you stretch your trusting wings
to rise in the elated freedom
of your newborn self.

HIDDEN FORESTS

We may dress up our wishes
with well-designed expectations,
visualize our desires
with fine details of entitlement.
But our genuine longing
stands naked in our heart,
eager only to embrace
what our nature will reveal.

We are unexpected forests
hidden under the skin of the desert,
packed into invisible seeds
of lavish imagination.
We wait to sprout in unforeseen ways,
transform into new shapes and colors,
expressing our authentic intentions
from the blueprint in our soul.

We are called upon, like musicians
from the womb of silence,
to compose new symphonies
with visions of beauty and light.

We pioneer the emerging wisdom
that is in our purpose to learn,
in our destiny to embody,
etching through our choices
the collective human message
on the walls of our time.

THE PATH OF THE HEART

Live your life
like you'd never have it
any other way.
Be amazed by it
like you have never seen
any of it before.
Honor your lessons and choices
as if they were the skillful hands
entrusted to sculpt your spirit.

Be present unto your breath,
transparent unto your heart.
Lean into each experience,
each moment in your journey,
as if they were intimate doorways
to your innermost treasures.

Lay down your outdated fears
at each new dawn of courage,
and your self-judgments
in the embrace of your compassion.

Love all that you are,
at all times, in all places,
all the way into your soul.

Let both your thoughts
and your feelings
be the stretching arms
welcoming wisdom into your life.
Let your intentions
and your experiences
weave into each other
like threads of synergy
in the unfolding art
of your becoming.

On the path to the heart of life,
let your heart do the walking.

SYNCHRONICITY

Synchronicity in soul's eye view
is not a blind coincidence.
Magic is no longer an illusion,
nor serendipity a stroke of luck,
when you choose to open wide
the windows of your heart.

Within the infinite field
of your open possibilities,
your inner windows are facing
the direction of your wisest choices.
When you listen closely
to your heart's discernment,
and sense the delicate rhythm
of events and lessons in your life,
you will begin to hear
the language of your soul,
and the wisdom it whispers from within.

The intensity and tenderness
of your life patterns and lessons
are the waves of your transformation.

They carry in their surge the potential
of people, events, and situations
that are called to land on your shore.
Your inner world and outer world
are the two dancers of your life,
whirling in each other's beat.

The dance is not only in the waves,
and its music not only in the breeze.
Look to the ocean that sends them all,
and its alignment with your inner call.
Dive deeper into your awareness
to see with the eyes of your soul,
how intently the threads of grace
are spun in the fabric of your life.

The weaver is also the musician,
and the lover
in whose heart you blossom
to the fullness of your being.

COMPASSION

Compassion is the sweet sound
of sacred bells in your heart,
the intoxicating aroma
of ancient flowers in your soul.
It is the glow of your higher nature,
and the guardian of your dignity.

It surges like an instinct from the deep,
and in its compelling presence
all else will vanish.
It may not be your first choice,
but once chosen,
it will be your only one.

Never turn your back
on the voice of your compassion.
It is your essence that forever
will remain unfettered by this world.

In the wake of your compassion,
you too will be transformed.

as it shines like a nurturing sun
in the sky of your giving,
and its warmth returns all things
back to their simple nature.

Compassion is your noble heart,
the one pulsating
in the chest of the great spirit,
where all beings of all life
gather to kindle their love.

When you make your home
in this house of love,
compassion becomes
the single window
through which you will view
and understand this world.

How Lovers Awake

Life presents a thousand mirrors
for your learning,
but your own heart is the seer.
Dancers, actors and warriors,
join you on your long journey
of quest and discovery,
and still, alone you enter
the inner gates of your knowing.

In all the eyes
you have been mining for love,
and in all the hearts
you have sought your validation,
it was your own soul that awaited you.
And in her silence,
she has honored each of your choices,
and planted them all like seeds
in the gardens of your transformation.

This is how lovers awake –
deep in the stillness of their soul.

One dream at a time,
one lesson, one insight,
with each caressing breath
melting upon their heartbeat.

They whirl in the winds of fate,
tearing their illusion
into the bareness of their spirit,
until no veils are left in their heart
to separate their visible world
from the invisible realms of their soul.

THE COMPASS IN YOUR SOUL

Whatever needs remembering,
will one day be forgotten.
But what is truly inspired
by the insistence of the soul,
will endure.

The choices that come from the deep
will complete the work of the heart.
When the structures of your mind
yield to the simple flow of living,
you come alive.

Your authenticity
is an intimate atmosphere
embracing your inner core.
This is where you truly thrive,
and where you grow the gardens
of your dearest aspirations.

The compass in your soul
is an instinct of consciousness.

It discerns a truer north,
invisible to your logic,
and points in the direction
of your higher nature.

Do not hesitate to be different.
You were deliberately created
to be you.
You may never really fit in,
but then, who does, and what for?

We are not here to preserve the façade
of a mask that will never see its face.
Be truly and deeply who you are –
this is the way you share your light,
the way you make the difference.

CHAPTER 5

Treasures in the Dark Night

Look down to your giant feet
as they walk the path of your soul.
Look at your keen artist's hands
as they sculpt your visions into life.
Your greater self
is no higher than your heart,
and your cherished purpose
no farther than your breath.

STRENGTH OF KINDNESS

In the hardest moments
of your darkest night,
choose kindness
as the first impulse of your heart.
It may not repel
the shadows engulfing you,
but it will shine its lucid beam
upon who you truly are.

It is not only the darkness
we need freeing from,
but the judgments in our own minds,
imprisoning our wounded hearts.
The walls of fears and resentment
are always locked from the inside.
Be infinitely kind with yourself –
be the first to see
and understand your pain.

Kindness is patient, mindful,
and thoroughly revealing.

Like a friendly dawn,
it will unveil your new reality,
and sit with you upon the horizon,
awaiting the rising of your light.

And when your heart awakens
to bring forth your dreams into life,
kindness will become
your guardian rock –
the authentic instinct
by which you will walk your talk.

FACING YOUR SHADOWS

If you can face your shadows
while still wearing your light,
gaze into the deep dark eyes
of your deepest fears,
while breathing love in forgiveness,
you will grow wings of inspired virtue.

You will rise with new strength
from your shadows to your light,
and surge into the sky of hope
with the boldness of a free heart.

You will build palaces of beauty
from the ashes of your ruins,
and send rivers of kindness
down the valleys of your grief.

If you can search deeply
the caves of your dark night,
and find the glow of compassion
in the womb of your agony…

If you can embrace a love
that knows no shame or judgment,
and accept the deepest loss
with no shreds of resentment...

You will ascend from your night
with the spirit of a fearless lion,
learn wisdom from the angels
and endurance from the stars.

In your shadows hide the treasures
you are yet to unveil with your love –
a light you must first be ready to own.

NEVER GIVE UP

Even in your hardest times,
never ever give up.
Your soul is a living well
of unlimited virtues,
of gifts surging from the deep
with vigorous abundance.

Learn the lessons you must,
but heal your wounded trust.
Nurture courage in your heart,
and let hope expand your view.
Your life is as flexible
as a miracle,
forever open as a first love.

Where you now walk,
you have not dwelt before.
You have crossed your own horizons,
and are now free to define your path.
Know you are loved beyond reason,
and that your journey will not fail.

Know you are empowered by life itself,
and that the universe is on your side.

What lies ahead is yet to unfold,
but as you have arrived all the way here,
trust that you are prepared and well suited
to pursue the call of your soul.

Own your true experience.
Wear it to create the destiny
that your soul has intended
in wearing you
as the body of her love.

NAVIGATING THE DARK NIGHT

Let not your wounds obstruct
what your love must now see.
Let not your fears override
what your heart already knows.

When the walls of your world
close in on you with rejection,
do not shrink into oblivion.
This is your moment to expand,
no matter how painful it feels.
It is here you stand your ground
and reach deeper into your soul.

When fate has you in her eclipse,
your heart would have you shine.
When one world would have you gone,
it's time to reach to a wider world.

From chaos rise with stronger spirit,
and in hardship nurture deeper love.
Into the embers of your broken heart
blow the breath of unyielding hope.

Find courage in your authentic voice
and passion in your ceaseless calling.
Your hour will be ascending
on the ever patient wheel of fortune.

The whisper of love may seem faint
in the battlefield of doubts –
in this twilight of your faith,
keep your ears closer to your heart.

See that you rise free
from the mud of resentment,
that you cross the corridors of pain
with lessons of compassion.

Learn to see clearly in the dark,
to discern your purpose in the mist.
Navigate this night
from the inside out,
and you will walk
the sweet path of love
with the winged feet
of your higher nature.

SOME TREES FALL

Some trees fall
to reveal the beauty of flowers.
Some buckets leak
to allow new raindrops to be gathered.
Some treasures are lost
for deeper gifts to be discovered.

And life never ceases to love,
even when your heart freezes.
The warm breath of the Great Spirit
will set new rivers free
out of the icy mountains,
and light will return to the valleys
with the delicate wings of butterflies.

When a tree falls,
the forest will carry its spirit
in the whisper of the wind.
It will guard its song among the leaves
that since forever have witnessed
each death giving birth to new life,

and each season inspiring
new bounty of love.

Too tender is your love.
So tender, it cannot diminish,
not even in the darkest dream.

Love forever remains awake
in the womb of the night.
In the soft veils of your longing,
it awaits its own ascent
at the dawn of your heart.

Wounds

These thoughts you hold on to
will keep wounding you
like rising labor contractions,
till you transform them into love.
Each single rock in you
that has been forged by pain
awaits being eroded
by the healing water of your soul.

Let this dark night reveal,
behind the veils of your anguish,
new treasures in your heart.
Let the emerging light
of your enduring nature,
filter into your awareness,
through the cracks of forgiveness
in the shell of your resentment.

Choose a higher road to lead you
out of the agony of this night.
Let it lift you to a taller sky,

where your wisdom has already laid
new pathways among the stars.

Nothing will ever make
the wrong become right,
yet your pain will turn to kindness
in your expanded heart.

From the intensity of your wounds,
you will grow gardens of compassion.
Freed by the power of your forgiveness,
you will know how deeply you are loved.

You Who Walk the Sky

If you cannot find your sun in the sky,
and your light has dimmed
to sunken worlds of memories,
look into the eyes of the moon.
It rises for you alone tonight,
stretching its silver invitation
across the ocean of your sadness.
For love only hides herself
as longing in your heart.
Her seeds are waiting there
only for your rain.

What was lost has not been buried.
Your dreams still stand on the horizon
like the spirits of your unborn gifts.
Their songs move through
the stillness in your heart,
like healing waves of hope
that will not stay away from shore.
They are so present in the wind,
even the mighty rocks can hear
the whisper of their passion.

If you cannot find your clarity
in your sky above,
look down to your giant feet
as they walk the path of your soul.
Look at your keen artist's hands
as they sculpt your visions into life.
Your greater self
is no higher than your heart,
and your cherished purpose
no farther than your breath.

In this night of your darkest hour,
you walk with none other than the stars.
In the vast space of your emptiness,
you are a glow of an ancient promise,
an emerging miracle of compassion –
the awakening of a human heart.

You were born in the arms of earth,
but your song has taken to the sky.
A lover of the highest nature,
your love knows not your fears.
Ride this night beyond its horizons
to worlds you are yet to create –
You who walk the sky.

THE PRAYER

Let all our heavy hearts,
burdened with grief and disbelief,
be carried by the inner eyelids,
whose innocence has gazed deeply
into the eyes of the darkest pain,
and seen the unfading glow of love.

Let this love send our tears
like thirsty waves of hope
to the shores of new visions,
to bays that are yet to tame
this restless ocean that we are.

There, in the water of forgiveness,
in the coves of reconciliation,
let the gracious spirits of the earth,
of the sky and of the sea,
bathe with our wounded souls
like playful dolphins of magic,
nurturing us with their compassion.

Let tenderness soothe our anguish,
and tolerance release our rage,
until all hearts are lighter than air,
all deeds have wings of kindness,
and we stand present
to our nature of love –
love that bears us all in her breath.

CHAPTER 6

Authenticity Rises at Dawn

*You do not awaken
by forsaking your dreams,
but by following the one dream
that is truly awake —
the one leading you to love.*

SOAR WITH THE WIND

Finding the passion in your soul,
and embracing your authenticity,
is where your dreams engage reality,
and where your efforts harvest
the rite of passage to your higher self.

This is where the creative force
of the abundant universe
bursts through your imagination,
inspiring your visions and gifts
to gather fragments of learning
into a masterpiece of destiny.

This is where your soul
truly touches the earth,
and with it touches the hearts
of all those you hold precious.
Love rains grace with its passion,
yet seeps deepest with authenticity.

Do not withhold your gifts in shyness,
nor hide your calling within your doubts.

Give all that wells from deep within you
the earnest voice of your days
and the silence of your nights,
so you yourself may see your virtues
and grow your courage in their light.

You are unique, different,
unusual and extraordinary.
Exhale your deepest song into the wind,
and soar with it to your higher heart.

YOUR HEART IS BORN FREE

This heart is born to be free.
You can cast it to the shadows
and it will return with wings.
You can throw it in the fire
and it will re-emerge as light.
You can judge and shame it
but its dignity will endure.
You cannot erase its nature,
nor imprison its untamed spirit.
It remains pure in this world,
raw in its bare simplicity,
its purpose rooted in your love,
its calling nested in your breath.

Your heart is wiser than knowledge,
as what it knows precedes thought.
It is clearer than all views,
as it sees all things from within.
At each dawn of transformation,
it rises like a gallant knight,
armed with unshakable virtues,
to discern hard and honest choices,
and stand by your higher nature.

Your free heart lives to be kind –
forever generous in love,
genuine in its compassion.
Its giving is true and abundant,
unfettered by cheat or deceit.
It has no walls and seeks no safety,
else its own inner strength.
It releases all fears and doubts
into the deep silence of trust,
and sets free all regrets
in the soft rivers of forgiveness.
In all ways, it seeks to inspire –
like the sun, nurture and heal,
like stars, glow in beauty of hope.

Let no one and nothing dim your light,
no judgment ever numb your calling.
Let your heart be the creative space,
where you assert your truth
and embody your freedom,
embracing your love and wisdom.

Wear your heart like it wears you –
the way the forest wears the wind
as it unleashes its spirit to the sky.

SCULPT YOUR DESTINY

Free yourself to your wider being,
and turn your fears into love.
Melt your pain into kindness,
and from struggles sculpt your strength.
You have sown the seeds of learning
all throughout your past.
Harvest in your fields the wisdom
of the lessons from your path.

Own your clarity
with the seniority of your soul.
Do not be disrupted
by the waves of changes,
as you have seen them all.
Claim with dignity
the ground of your experience,
and with passion,
the sky of your love for life.

Do not hold back –
be your endless self.

Let your freedom guide you
to the gifts of your birth.
Live the life of your choice,
and love the choices you are making.
Free of judgments,
rise bolder from your failures,
and wake up wiser
from your broken dreams.

Stand authentic by your truth,
steadfast by your purpose.
In the page-less book of life,
write the destiny of your own.
Seek not the approval of this world,
nor the safety of its protective walls.
Follow only your truest calling
with the compass of your heart.

On your edge of the universe
you are a pioneer of love –
claim your freedom to change the world.

The Dream that Will Awake You

Life is a river of lucid dreams.
You do not awaken
by forsaking your dreams,
but by following the one dream
that is truly awake –
the one leading you to love.

Authenticity rises at dawn.
If you let your heart be nowhere else
and nothing else but your true nature,
it will bloom into exquisite beauty,
exude like enchanted fragrances
into each space you have created
in the womb of your deepest dreams.

Authenticity awakens in you,
when the trumpets of this world,
and the drums of your ambitions,
fall silent in the simple presence
of the innocence in your heart.
It stands its ground between the pillars

of the darkness and the light,
like a threshold of higher knowledge
and the guardian of integrity.

When you finally detach
from your resistance to the changes,
you become like sand dunes in a desert –
willing to shape shift your formation
as often as your life requires,
knowing that your authentic essence
will prevail
as your eternal code of life.

IN YOUR TRUTH

You stand taller in your inner truth,
and nobler in your higher nature.
Let no one's shadows dwarf your gifts,
no disapproval unnerve your steps.
Walk with certainty in your heart,
even when your path withers from sight
in eerie mist of blame and rejection.
Let the deep knowing in your heart
be your eyes to discern your way.

When fate uproots you from your world,
do not linger in the ruins.
Be daring, even when your fears
catch up with you out of breath.
Your purpose and your gifts
are rooted deep within your soul,
and what awaits on your horizons
will, in time, dawn into your life.

Stand taller by your inner truth,
and make peace
with this crossroad on your path.

Where you are now is the vantage point
from which your soul observes your life.
This moment is one of authentic choices,
guided by the voice of your discernment.

Be willing to cast away your doubts
far behind your winged shoulders.
Find your strength in your inner truth,
as gifts ahead await your loving.
Stand tall and free by your heart –
nothing can stop your nature,
nor the passion of your calling,
from maturing into your light.

STAR SEEDS

Like shooting stars, we try so hard
to share our light with the world.
We blaze across many skies,
most of which are way too far,
too estranged from our native star.

We must shine first in our own sky,
see our glow with our inner eye,
rain our love on the thirsty fields,
where we grow seeds from our soul.

We must learn to fly like wild birds,
free of gravity, spared from doubts,
homebound, clear and undeterred,
navigating by an instinct of purpose
across the long shadows of old beliefs.

We are star seeds from the tree of life,
born in the Super Nova of souls.
Bearing in our light visions of change
and blueprints of a kinder world,
we are ambassadors of hope.

We are the ones
whom we promised ourselves
to meet in this land of destinies.
Each of us carries our unique glow,
but none can light the world alone.

Hang your star high in the sky –
you were called here by infinite love.
Embody the gifts that have you present,
and weave them softly
into the majestic fabric of creation.

SOUL PROMISE

It is the memory of a soul promise
that beckons your longing –
a soft persistent passion,
coded in the veins of your soul.
To choose to be fully here
and yield your heart to love,
is your irresistible urge of nature.

Your higher heart exudes
its compelling scent of wisdom,
calling in elated visions
from subtle, formless worlds.
Let this scent of purpose
roam the streets of your mind,
open wide gates of questions
in the city walls of set beliefs.

Choose to do what you love most,
and let love undo the rest.
Gather all your life lessons,
your gifts, your insights and dreams,

into a blooming bouquet of passion,
and hand it over to your heart.

Lay the burden of uncertainty,
the weight of all your worries,
and the shackles of your doubts
upon your mighty wings of trust,
where you own the power of your soul.

Spread your deepest prayers
and the crumbs of all your efforts
like petals on the path of love,
and watch your feet of gratitude
walk this bridge of promise
all the way to the sky.

At the Gates of Life

When you enter the stillness
in your breath,
and carve space for beauty
in your cluttered mind,
it rains harmony and blessings
in your thirsty heart.

These are the gates of life –
dormant magic awakened by love,
enchanted silence pregnant with grace,
the sweet glow of subtle wisdom,
where you meet, face to face,
the infinite presence of your soul.

You cannot shy away from this love,
nor hide in the safety of your thoughts,
as the winds of your awakening
have already brought down the house.

Let the buoyancy of your soul
lift you weightless in your trust,

elated in your clarity of purpose,
empowered by your light.

Like Earth, nurturing all life upon it,
be the spring of your own abundance.
With the flow of your surging passion,
grow jungles of kindness in your heart.

Free your spirit to the full expanse
of who you truly are.
This journey around the sun
is for souls dancing around love.

CHAPTER 7

Awake in
Both Worlds

*Live here, on the wings
of each instance of existence.
This is where eternity meets time,
and infinity cuddles the finite;
here, where your heart touches life,
and you kiss the face of grace.*

To Be Here

To be here
is to let the sky have bare feet,
beam eternity on the screen of time,
give wings to the dreams of earth,
soaring with our human songs
from the passion within our breath.

To be here
is to dress life's purest intention
with the bodies of human choices,
and to let love's timeless nature
whisper its clarity
in the inner rooms of our hearts.

You will find it
nowhere else but here.
This is the sacred threshold
of awakening –
the boat of wisdom
in the ocean of dreams,
where soul treasures are refined by earth,
and earth's longing embraces the sky.

In a single window
of a living moment,
eternity walks by time,
its dress lingers with the stars
like a trail of inner beauty,
caressing with a promise
the human longing
for their highest nature.

Wake up now,
the entire journey is unfolding
right in front of your soul's eyes.
You will know you are awake
when you are entranced by love.

I Love that You Are Nameless

I love that you are nameless,
so I can call you without words.
I love that you are weightless,
so I can fly within your heart
and you can be my wings.

I love that everywhere I look,
you paint your beauty in my eyes,
and every time I think of you
my heart melts my thoughts away,
transforming me to love.

I love that you are so present,
that with you my ego disappears,
so when we are alone together,
intimacy guards our space
and I can be fully here.

I love that you are timeless,
and that our time
is out of this space.

I used to walk on earth,
where I would look around for you.
Now I walk the sky,
where you look after me.

You are awake
in the silence in my heart.
How could I remain asleep,
when in your stillness
my soul dances with the stars?

THE INTUITIVE WEAVERS

Our intuitive perception,
the subtle bridge between dimensions,
is like a graceful hammock
stretching us between the worlds.
In its swing, we lay our hearts,
not so much to ponder our fate,
as to set free our awareness
from the web of time and space,
envision a kinder world emerging.

Silence runs through this golden thread,
flowing from our breath to the light,
and in it, the spontaneous knowing
that we exist in all dimensions.
Our thirst propels us through the veils
to the subtle realms of visions,
where we embrace
the fullness of our being.

Visions bloom in authenticity.
Let us see first that our soul

is indeed the seer,
that our bare feet of humility
firmly touch the earth,
and that our quest is truly guided
by sincerity in our hearts.

Like weavers of the invisible,
we braid the purest of intentions
with the discernment we have earned
through our shared human learning.
Far enough into the passage
of evolution from fear to love,
we have come to see our freedom
as life's deep belief in us –
trusting we will grow to choose the light.

Let us not override
these precious visions in our hearts,
just because they are yet to cross
from imagination into life,
from intentions into deeds,
and from potential
to the honest harvest
of our collective labor of love.

IN THE RIVER OF CHANGE

Everybody wants to manifest a dream.
We live our hopes and wishes
through a flux of life lessons,
bound in the ceaseless river of change.

You cannot control this river's course,
and everything you place in its flow,
in time, will be devoured by
its insatiable hunger for change.
Such is the nature of dreaming,
the fabric of its elusive existence.

But you can choose
what matters most to your soul.
And, if dream you must,
it is well you dream of what you love,
and long for its presence in your heart.

It is from these dreams you awake
to become the magical instrument
of love's native essence,
in this auditorium of time and space.

The timeless core of all love,
untouched by the chaos of this world,
rests in the stillness of your soul.
It incubates in the silence
like the first anticipating note
of the finest celestial music.

It is from here you rise to play
the elated symphony of life,
emerging into your brilliance –
stars applauding,
angels rising to their feet.

The Un-Manifested

The unchangeable essence
of all that is,
remains un-manifested.
This is how it stays outside
of the eternal cycle of change.
Resting in the womb of the present,
all things pass by its window,
as it forever observes their flow.

It embraces the entire universe
from within the heart of life,
witnessing its evolution
from outside of time and space.
Everything spins around it
in an eternal creative dance,
yet, it remains forever still.

It listens from this stillness
to all the songs and prayers,
born from the first sounds of life.
But its original silent wave

remains untouched and unchanged,
transforming the whole creation
without ever altering itself.

We whisper this enigma
like a legend through the ages.
Yet, this is only half the secret.
This half can become transparent
to an innocent open heart.

The other half is the endless quest
to embody this in our lives.
Through all the trials and the changes,
staying true to this essence,
free and genuine in our detachment,
while embraced in its enchantment,
like miracles of the deepest love
that are as simple
as a single breath.

THE TOWER OF GRACE

Between the epiphany of hindsight
and the uncertainty of foresight,
rises a tall tower of grace,
asserting each present moment
as a gate to limitless awareness.

Free from the chains of the past,
unburdened by the weight of the future,
this inspired threshold of presence
flows like a miracle through life,
its clarity carried in the wind
like a floating portal in time.

A single window, empowered
by the transparency of being,
open into worlds free of beliefs,
where life unfolds as creative waves
in the sea of endless potential.

Live here, on the wings
of each instance of existence.

This is where eternity meets time,
and infinity cuddles the finite;
here, where your heart touches life,
and you kiss the face of grace.

Lean into each present moment
like a lover,
embracing each curve of experience
into the spiral of your learning,
and let your loving tower the stars.

MY SOUL STAR

This golden cord of light
that bonds me with your presence
is where my breath begins.
Invisible to my eyes,
yet transparent to my heart,
you are the timeless in my space,
and I am your moment here.

You are the ancient magic
wizards have called to earth,
the alchemists have sought,
and sages have revealed.

You are my higher nature –
I wear you as my crown,
and you wear me as your body.
In silence you are a whisper,
and in your whispers
you are my wisdom.

I breathe you into my thirst,
and your fragrance is the air
sharing secrets in my lungs
in the atmosphere of love
encircling my heart.

You are a guardian of mysteries,
the gates of higher knowledge.
You surface like a miracle
in everything I see.
Your light inspires music
of infinite notes of kindness,
you draw from instruments of nature,
and spread across my path
like petals of compassion.

You are my beloved soul star,
home to my highest hope,
the DNA of my journey
and the signature of love,
etched like a seal of purpose
into each thread of my life.

THE VEILS ARE THIN NOW

Do not hold back
when love beckons you
deep into her lucid lakes,
where ethereal light beings
dance through her silky veils.

Embrace her presence
when your longing
rises with her breath,
expanding into the light,
drawing visions from her silence,
as new horizons for your life.

Be fully here
when your soul reveals to you
the secrets of her original design.
The veils are thinning now,
but forever will elude your mind;
let go to your tenderness,
to the lucent softness of your heart.

Find the gentle strings
of your emerging music

in your ascending violin,
and the lyrics of your love
that soon you will be singing
from new stages in your life.

Look deeper through these veils –
the ancient light symbols
rising from inner wells
are gifts from worlds beyond.
The wisdom calling in the mist
is whispered by your soul –
your thirst has turned to water
in the intensity of your love.

For so long you have walked
like a nomad between the worlds.
Now the worlds draw nearer
as you come closer to your heart.
The veils are growing thinner,
your mind silenced by your trust.

When love beckons you from the deep,
dive into her lucid lakes.
Dive as far as your lungs can take it,
until gratitude becomes your breath.

CHAPTER 8

The Intimate Planet of Love

When you see
a bit of me in you,
and I see a bit of you in me,
and we find nothing to judge,
only a lot to learn,
and everything to love –
then Life itself does the seeing.

OUR PLANET OF LOVE

To love
not only the lovable in you,
but that which most needs loving.

To see you
not only for your beauty,
but also for the rose that grows
from your pain to your light.

To listen not only
to your wisdom and laughter,
but also to your burdened heart,
as it strives to free you
from lingering cords of the past.

To melt our hearts together
into a river of gratitude,
born from our transparency
in the mirror of our love.

To commit our souls
through the corridors of fears

to the giants of love that we are,
even as we struggle
in the cocoon of our becoming.

To mindfully walk together
upon the infinitely delicate line
between our shadows and our light.

To nurture each other's calling
through the ripening of our sharing,
and then harvest with grace
the sweet fruits of love's work,
as we courageously create
our intimate planet of love.

YOUR TRUE ALLY

Do not resist
the mirror she holds
to your vulnerable heart.
Do not deny
the murky water she uncovers
among the shadows of your mind.

She cannot help but be the waves,
cuddling with her empathy
the rocky shores of your pride.
She won't stop raining honesty
on your mountains of defiance,
and with her tenderness erode
the stubborn walls in your heart.

As if she were the essence
of magical healing flowers,
she flows in your restless veins
like oxygen in wasted rivers.
She is your Delphic Priestess,
a goddess from ancient tales,
the feminine mirror to your soul.

From within the glow of her beauty
and the precious eyes you adore,
from beneath the softness of her touch
and the playful curls in her laughter,
she rises like a storm
behind the veils of your mind.

Powerful, on her horse of freedom,
a fierce warrior of the heart,
she is your truthful ally.
She will ride the distance with you
to the lands of your higher calling,
as you will ride with her
to the fields of her destiny.

If you let her do so,
she will shatter your armor
and free your heart to the sun
with the spear that once pierced her spirit,
long ago, very long ago,
when you hurled it to the sky
with the intensity of your prayers
in your blazing longing for true love.

THE INTIMACY OF AWAKENING

How I love to turn my heart
to the glow of your moonlit face,
hear the stars rolling in your laughter,
breathe the sweetness of your embrace.

To send my spirit diving
in the crystal pools of your beauty,
melt like tears in the tender grace
that has become home to our love.

How precious are the years
and all their gifted little moments,
in which we share not only our dreams,
but the intimacy of our awakening.

Each conscious step we have taken
to be transparent with our souls,
has nurtured forests in our love.
Each moment of being present
to each other's unfolding journeys,
has fused the atmospheres of our hearts.

I swam with you in your sadness,
and you stood by me through my pain.
We learned to hear each other's silence,
and dance our hearts into rain.
Nurtured upon the tree of life,
we have become precious flowers
of the kindness woven in our love.

Cuddled like the earth and sky
in our space of tenderness,
the subtle veils between our souls
have turned to eyelids
on the soft angels' faces,
through which we see each other's hearts,
and embrace
the fullness of our love.

WINGS OF SPIRIT

How beautiful are the wings
of freedom in your soul,
that send your heart soaring
into the luminous sky
of unconditional love.

Do not wait
for life to shed her skin
before you meet your spirit,
nor seek her secrets in
your thoughts and your dreams.
But rest your mind
deep within your breath,
and feel your nature
within its silent embrace.

Anchor deep in your heart
the roots of your tree of life.
Let each of your soul gifts
ripen on your tall branches,
and each of your insights
nest in your lavish foliage.

Grow your wings strong and wide,
while you are still alive,
while your soul can touch the earth
and spring your visions into life.

And send your heart flying
to define a wider sky
for each of your hopes
with the maturity of your love.

Whatever comes your way,
do not lose sight of love.
Let nothing and no one
hide this magic
from your unwavering heart.

You are a planet of love.
Be relentlessly and persistently
the unconditional magnificent you.

BOUNDLESS PRESENCE OF LOVE

Love ascends from the deep,
like a breath unfolding to life.
Its surging beauty moves like waves
through the stillness of your being,
spreading kindness over your shores.

But when your life must transform,
love will become a fierce storm.
It will wreak havoc in your shadows,
and through the chaos send you spinning,
all the way to your new beginning.

You do not own love,
nor does love wish to own you.
It takes residence in your heart,
so you can become a home
to your own higher nature,
and savor the virtue of your gifts.

Love is authenticity
in its original form.

It stands by your calling
and nurtures your passion.
It is who you truly are
in your purest state of being –
too subtle for your thoughts,
too alive to judge your choices.

It would be wise to let love
navigate the course of your heart,
and entrust to it the secrets
of your innermost dreams.

Somewhere along our journey,
we all come to understand
that love is more than a wonder
appearing on our path of life.
Rather, it is life that is unfolding,
like a ripple of awareness,
within the boundless presence of love.

SOUL FRIENDSHIPS

The sweetest friendship is the one
that mirrors your bond with your heart.
It springs like a fountain from the deep,
its beauty wearing love as wings.
It carries the essence of hope,
like grace into your spaces of grief,
weaving its presence in your heart
with threads of genuine listening.

You spend the long nights together,
not to wallow in your pain,
nor to linger in your doubts.
Your sharing is fearlessly honest,
stirring your passion with visions,
rooted in the calling of your souls.

Let this friendship be
transparent and free,
with all the doors of your hearts
open in both directions,
so you may grow your corridors of trust
into palaces of integrity.

Let there be no dimming of the light,
only delight in each other's virtues,
the selfless sharing of your gifts,
strengthening each other's hearts,
and uplifting each other's spirits.

Equal in giving and receiving,
infused by dignity and respect,
let each of your eager hearts
soar with your own voices,
adding your own lyrics
to the songs you create together.

These are the friendships endowed to us,
both by destiny and choice in our hearts.
Timid they may enter our space,
yet authentic they grow in our lives.
On their precious trusted bridges,
we meet not only each other,
but forever approach our souls
to deepen our bond with our nature,
awaking in unconditional love.

LOVE REVEALS HERSELF

I have stood forever on the shores
of my awareness, yearning for you.
I searched and prayed for your presence,
and in my thirst awaited your grace,
but it was deep within my heart
that you first showed your true face.

Like a fragrance from secret gardens
buried deep in my soul,
you ascended,
wafting like a wind in my forests,
touching every leaf with your whisper,
flickering in every ray of my trust,
melting like a taste of pure beauty
on the eager lips of my heart.

I knew you were coming to me
like a mist from the valleys of fate,
and even before I saw you,
your presence was there at my gate,
as if it were a faint silhouette
of how precious you'd become to me.

I have slowed down to zero
in my longing to catch up with you.
I have emptied my life in the mirror
to make space for this dream to come true.
And it was from the stillness in my breath
that you rose like a precious first star
on the horizons of my inner sky.

I have no name with which to call you now,
as you wear so many names in our minds.
I have no frame to hold your image,
as you are formless within my heart.
You are my life in its purest intention,
the essence of truth in all my expressions,
and in each kind moment of attention,
you unveil like reality from a dream.

Let us not sleep in this hour,
when every string in our hearts
quivers with this enchanting call.
Love reveals herself like a fragrance;
breathe her and embrace her
all the way to your heart and soul.

EYES OF THE HEART

The Heart is the window
through which we can see
ourselves in each other,
and look deeply into
the wider nature of life
in all its ways of being.

When you see
a bit of me in you,
and I see a bit of you in me,
and we find nothing to judge,
only a lot to learn,
and everything to love –
then Life itself does the seeing.

This is when we awake
to the true nature of Self.
This is where we stand with dignity
by each other's truth,
and expand the circle of our being
to include all life, in all its expressions,
and its diversity of visions and dreams.

When a flower longs to fly,
it entrusts its grace to a butterfly.
When humans long to evolve,
they turn towards love –
love that embraces all dimensions
and dwells in all worlds.

Do not let this simple beauty
fly by you, invisible to your eyes.
Be awake in your listening space
to hear the footsteps of love,
even before she knocks
on the thirsty doors of your heart.

CHAPTER 9

Creative Wings
of Vision

Every vision takes her first breath
in our fields of imagination.
She learns to walk in our thoughts
when we give her legs of trust.
Then we grow our wings of passion
and she teaches us how to fly
from the little rooms in our mind
to new freedom in her wider sky.

THE ARCHER

You are an archer of intentions,
a hunter of the invisible,
a sculptor of timeless visions.
But you are also a student of life,
a prayer in search of a form,
a song still being composed.

The passion in your heart's calling,
the highest aim of your inner sight,
and the stillness in your breath,
must all be firmly aligned
to your clear focus of intention,
when launching your arrow of vision
to complete the purpose in your soul.

Among all that you choose to do,
there is one thing you must undo –
exhale all that is no longer you.
Empty your space for the new event
that is to become your presence,
and stretch the bow of your will
with love for the life you assert.

Then, inspired by the wisdom
harvested through your life lessons,
and by the innate buoyancy
of your invincible spirit,
free your wings to carry your vision,
and fly forward into space
like eternity into time.

IF YOUR SONG IS AWAKE

The visions that have crystallized
in the caves of your longing,
release them from the ancient rocks
that have nested their spirits,
and free them to the open valleys
of your life's playing.

If the song in your heart is awake,
it is time to abandon
your hatching ground.
It is time to spread wide
the wings of your soul,
follow your heart's instinct
with the passion of your inner call,
and carry your music
to the ears of the sky.

The timing of your destiny
is as imminent as your choice.
Be awake at the dawn of your heart.
The fears you have braved

through the darkness of the night
must now give way to your light.

Own your strength with authority,
and leap like a wild lion
into your wider nature –
where you belong,
where you thrive,
and where you matter.

Your creativity is the way
your soul nature talks to the world.
You may learn the skills,
but the language is innate.

WHEN CHANGE CALLS YOU

If what you see in the world
tears the fabric of your spirit
and breaks your heart into
unbearable human pieces,
know that in your pain lives
the hidden calling of your soul.

A fierce compassion
in the womb of your deepest nature,
rising like a healer from your wounds.

A genuine clarity,
born of your innate discernment,
seeing with the eyes of wisdom
through the veils of deception.

To be awake where others sleep,
to fearlessly assert
and call into the light
that which now must change.

Do not hold back the visions
that are born from your instinct of love,
flourishing like forests in your heart,
charging forth like warriors of integrity.

True change is not born of systems,
nor will it prevail by force.
It is triggered in the hearts of people,
labored through their struggles and choices,
maturing in the passion of their souls.

Visions Fly in Trust

Visions are born in seeing
into subtle worlds of potential,
but they live to be seen in this world.
Even the stars blink with some doubt,
as they blaze in their passion,
and still they send their light
across the distance of time and space
like relentless beacons of hope.

Never silence the whisper
of your heart's innermost calling.
In the whirling of your emotions,
on the dance floor of your choices,
the music of your higher heart
will reveal its nature to the light.
In its unveiling you'll grow in trust.

Dance your visions all the way to life,
even when no one else is dancing,
even when only the invisible
applauds the promise of your song
and believes in your potential.

What now still walks in your dreams
will one day be the powerful wings
that will carry you in your purpose.

It has taken the labor of self-love
to give birth to your precious visions.
It will be the courage of self-belief
that will free them from the cage of doubts.
Tomorrow belongs to new worlds,
whose hearts now call you in your dreams.

The winds of grace are the face
of a freedom native to life.
They blow in the direction of love,
and carry each seed of human faith
on its unyielding flight of purpose.

If you show up on this flight,
you will live to see destinies
glowing with invincible light,
flared by visionary abundance,
born from many hearts like yours
that braved the sky to rise with trust.

THE HUMAN ARTIST

Nothing can give form to visions
better than the loving hands
of hearts that dream them into being.
No one is worthier to sing this song
than the voice of the one
who carries its music in her heart.

The human artist is
her own unfinished painting.
She works to complete herself
through each brushstroke of choice.
Her only true audience
is the very life she paints
through the lessons of her soul.

In her craft, she has a thousand ways
to sculpt this wonder of existence.
With the eyes of her poised heart
she gives shape to the formless,
even before its stillness awakes.
In her intuitive, open windows

she sees love already dancing
to the tunes she has yet to compose.

But it is her bold passion
that propels forward her will,
that drives her imagination,
giving birth to each step she takes.
The space her visions create
define her boundaries of fate,
and into this creative space
she sets her spirit free.

Defying fears, she paints her destiny
from the love surging in her soul –
love that will unveil as her art
and the gift of mastering her heart.

VISIONS BELONG TO LIFE

Every vision takes her first breath
in our fields of imagination.
She learns to walk in our thoughts
when we give her legs of trust.
Then we grow our wings of passion
and she teaches us how to fly
from the little rooms in our mind
to new freedom in her wider sky.

We stretch our hearts to fly with her,
but she is larger than our dreams,
and the hour will come
for her to claim her own adventure.

She wants to fly in future skies
that we cannot even perceive.
She longs to glow in new worlds,
far beyond our boundaries.

The deepest visions in our hearts
do not belong to us alone.

Long ago, they stood with us,
as we ourselves wished for form.

They are the gifts of life's genius,
the offer of her compassion.
When we are aligned in our intentions,
we become their true expressions.

The visions that will change our lives
belong to life.
They are instruments of evolution
that we ourselves are now a part of.
Like seeds of a destined future,
they will sprout
wherever they find
a fertile ground.

THE MUSE ON THE HORIZON

The muse in your soul
is the radiance of your inner sun
just before it reaches the horizon
to ascend in your conscious mind.

It is your well of wisdom,
the invisible magician
deep within your breath,
inspiring creative visions
with exuberant fountains
among the mountains of your thoughts.

These visions are not meant to hang
on the inner walls of your heart.
You cannot hide them behind
your curtains of uncertainty.
The only reason the sky stretches
from horizon to horizon
is its yearning to be lit
by unlimited possibilities.

Let your visions fly
like kisses of hope from your lips,
reverberate like songs of change
in your self-empowered voice.

Let them take like butterflies
into the early morning breeze,
and spray colors of new realities
across the skeptical fields
of this embattled, thirsty world.

THE FLUTE OF LOVE

It is hard to understand
why human souls
will pack so much hate
into their fate,
and store so many fears
behind their tears,
when even the simple sky
will stretch forever
to make room for love.

When we exhale our pain
through the holes in our heart
into music of forgiveness,
and then allow each emptiness
lingering within
to be filled by silence –
we become a flute of love
in the masterful hands
of life's compassion.

In the human heart,
hope is the eye of the soul.

It sees not only what is,
but what we long to become.
It is the maturity of our love
that awakens our hope into visions,
and our appreciation of life
that stirs our visions into actions.

Let our actions be the music
of compelling generosity
and of sweet kindness of hearts.
Let them rise from the flutes of love
that more of us are now becoming,
sensitive instruments of change,
boldly rising from their pain
to rewrite the destiny of mankind.

CHAPTER 10

The Kindness of Self-Love

Do not judge what needs to be loved,
nor shame what needs your compassion.
Love especially those parts in you
that are most difficult to love.
Even your shadows long for your light,
and in them are your hidden treasures.

THE EXQUISITE RELIEF

The exquisite relief
in loving who you are,
the elated simplicity
of accepting where you are,
and the wisdom to let go
of everything else.

The magnificent clarity
of being no greater and no less
than the song you carry in your heart.
Your destiny is not yet sealed,
and your story awaits its completion.
New visions will emerge from the mist,
deeper gifts will seek your awareness,
and your passion will blaze new paths.

But in this present moment here,
you are cuddled in the arms of life –
loving who you have become,
free from the cords of your past,
as you stand vulnerable and real
in the naked view of your heart.

To embrace your intimate nature,
and love each sparkle and wrinkle
in the honest way you show up.
Powerful in your free will,
sincere in your way of caring,
unpretentious in your sharing.
Too simple to hide your dreams,
too authentic to deny your truth,
too open to judge your choices.

Nothing can inspire you more
and court such greatness from your heart,
as loving yourself to this freedom
of owning who you are,
and unveiling your full nature to the light.

My Love Affair with Life

You and I are lovers,
never to be seen.
Our intimate affair
is out of this world.
We belong in no story
and may never be remembered.
The proof of your existence
is your presence in my heart.

You surround me like the air
around the empty space
of a breath longing to be taken.
I embrace you into me,
as a heart would welcome
the soft knocking of its beat.
I climb the windows of my thirst
to spend my nights with you,
and wake up from my dreams
when you dawn in my awareness.

I sneak through the veils,
homebound to worlds of magic,

as you whisper me all the way here
to a new day of awakening.
How fortunate that we share
only one pair of wings,
and in flying to our love,
you guide me from within.

I open my heart to you,
as a flower would to the light,
not so much to show,
as to be nurtured by your sight.
Transparent in your kindness
are your wide open windows,
these long lucid tunnels
so embedded in my soul,
where forever I approach you
like a lover to his inner call.

Freedom in Forgiveness

It matters not how right or wrong you are;
forgiveness is always larger than both.
It is hard to forgive
what pains you the most.
But from the viewpoint of a lifetime,
it is always more hurtful
not to forgive.

Forgiveness is the fruit
of growing to your size of love.
It doesn't redress the wrong,
but it will melt your poison away.
It lets the river of your heart
scrape clean its banks of resentment,
and the winds of changing seasons
carry away your leaves of regret.

To face your hardest memory
and release it in your self-love.
To free space for new learning
from within the despair of grief,

and commit to new horizons
in the view of your higher heart.

Then, to witness with clearer eyes
a love that has no memories,
free and buoyant like a fresh breath,
powerful and bold like the early sky,
creating from the air of forgiveness
an atmosphere for a newborn world
that now exists only in your dreams.

SELF-LOVE

Self-love,
one of life's deepest lessons,
is at your highest call of faith.
No matter how many times
you've seen your world fall apart,
tossed in space by brutal fate,
wobbling in your painful doubts,
there is always a new sun rising
on the skyline of your heart,
lighting up your world with trust.

Sweetness is born with the dawn
of each courageous new beginning –
when you can finally embrace
all you have been to this moment,
all you have learnt and created,
lost, abandoned or hated,
choosing now to love it all
into your wakeful, wiser soul.

Self-love – a virtue
both innate and chosen,

the way you opt to stand
by your authentic nature.
It is the backbone of free will –
your deep soul commitment
to rise above the culture
of unconsciousness and resentment.

Awakened journeys do not endure
in victimhood and self-pity.
You claim the reins of your destiny
when you assert your honest truth,
stand by your self-worth and values,
boldly draw your explicit boundaries
of integrity and self-love.

Never dim the light in your heart.
Let nothing in this world blind you,
nor eclipse your inner knowing
of how special and unique you are.
Love what you have in your soul,
and you'll have all that love offers.
Be forever,
fully and relentlessly,
the simple and magnificent you.

BEAUTY GLOWS IN THE DEEP

Oh, beauty of the soul,
dancing among the wrinkles
of long and well earned journeys,
ascending like silence from the deep
to tame the waves of restless hearts.

You shine your wisdom
in the healing eyes of compassion.
In this tired world of pain and strife,
your soft glow on the face of life
restores our faith in human dignity.

Your presence needs no words
to complete the work of the soul.
Like a mirror of love in stillness,
you rest outside of time and space,
reflecting back our higher nature.

Oh, beauty of the soul,
you embrace all prayers,
and the hearts who send them,

back to the hidden answers
within our own yearning.

Like a graceful moon in the
thickest hours of the night,
you rise as self-love in our sky
to paint a silver path of hope
upon our human bay of longing,
where ships of kinder worlds
will one day drop their anchors –
a vision only eyes of love can see,
and only innocence can draw in.

EMPOWERED SELF

Where you are now is your reality,
not where you should or could have been.
You are always at your creative edge
in the present seat of your soul's learning.
You'll find no triumphs in fighting yourself –
only humiliated victims of self defeat.

What was lost needs your releasing,
as in your grief new love is nesting.
What was taken by the call of fate
will grow taller in your resilience,
and kinder worlds will be created
from the authenticity in your heart.

Do not judge what needs to be loved,
nor shame what needs your compassion.
Love especially those parts in you
that are most difficult to love.
Even your shadows long for your light,
and in them are your hidden treasures.

And what are these shadows within us,
but cages for all that needs our loving –

abandoned fragments of our spirit,
trapped in floating bubbles of illusion,
yearning to emerge back to our light?

All your doings, right and wrong,
your greatest and worst choices,
all mistakes and their learning,
all have been instruments of love –
carving space for greater freedom,
and new depth for inner wisdom.

See it now from your soul's eye view,
embrace your journey in your heart.
Forgive your pain into compassion,
your regrets into acceptance,
and love your life to its full expression.

Like a lion in its wilderness,
stand empowered by your nature.
Your home is not the streets of doubt,
but the open fields of new adventures.
Define not your sky by your beliefs –
let it unfold from your own love's call
as it rises from deep within your soul.

FACE YOUR LIGHT

Face your light to see your nature –
all of your light –
even your soft vulnerable glow
in the crystal caves of your longing,
and in the shadows of your wounds.

You are the dancing shoreline
between strength and sensitivity,
courage and fear, wisdom and doubt.
In you, infinity meets the finite
and shadows find their light.

Your radiant heart extends to the sky,
yet is nurtured by your deepest roots.
Visions you send flying high
were fashioned in the mud
of your human transformation.

Face all of your light to find your song,
as wholeness is your house of knowledge.
Do not live by ideas and beliefs,

let no self-judgment obstruct your soul –
see all that you are, and love it all.

Listen deeply to your heart's whisper,
do not hold back your inner passion.
Embody your nature as your purpose,
and let your true gifts be your sharing.

The deeper you look into your soul,
the further you will travel in love.

INSTINCT OF AUTHENTICITY

Self-love is rooted in your instinct,
in your authentic presence here,
in the knowing of who you are,
beneath your self-doubt and fear.

Self-love is not selfish,
yet filled with self respect.
It is not about your ego,
but your true expansive self.

Look deeper into your heart,
you'll be amazed by what you find.
Do not wait until the end
to meet the magic of your soul.

Do not anticipate others
to validate your worth,
nor acknowledge the gifts
that you yourself must embrace.

Your longing is your mirror
for the face of your integrity.
You are wired straight to love
by your instinct of authenticity.

Be as genuine as the essence
of all that defines your nature.
You are a version of the divine,
a spark of its infinite light.

When you learn to love yourself,
you find this light all around you –
a presence of a subtle oneness
weaving all existence in a vine,
erasing the illusion of otherness
with awareness of a root design.

This is life's original intent,
love in its purest essence –
the human and the divine,
entwined in the cycle of creation,
bonded in the circle of inclusion
of all life in its diversity of forms.

Never separated, never away,
you rise like a wave in your boundless self,
a spontaneous ripple of self-awareness,
forever spreading through the heart of love.

CHAPTER 11

The Weightless Symphony of Being

*Each gentle breath touching your heart
with the magic of becoming you,
is the way you fall in love with life,
and the truest way for life itself
to live and love, and create through you.*

YOUR FREQUENCY IS YOUR SONG

The frequency of your love
is your authentic sound,
the one growing in your heart
to become your living song.
You abundantly share it,
often unknowingly,
and it touches many hearts,
even with no echo in return.

Your lyrics may still be forming,
some notes are yet to be composed,
but the music in your heart ascends
from the frequency in your soul.
Your song is as unique
as your very essence.
It is your signature in space,
the gift you share with the world.

Lovers find themselves
in the intimacy of their love.
Poets find their words
in the silence of their soul.

You find the completion of your song
in the contractions of your growth,
as what you sing to the world,
you must first fully own yourself.

Your frequency will mature to music,
and you will first hear it in your life.
Listen closely until you are ready,
until you have quieted your mind.
It is then that Love will pick you
as her favorite violin,
and each fiber in your heart
will be her quivering string.

On the horizons of our time,
I see souls gathering around.
They sing of love and beauty,
each in their own unique sound.
Their harmony caresses
both the darkness and the light,
their music melts down the walls
that for ages have divided our hearts.

LIVING AN INSPIRED LIFE

Live an inspired life
from the roots of your love
to the wings of generosity.
Explore uncharted oceans
from the shores of your longing
to the horizons of your calling.

Be weightless in your joy
and brave through your sorrow,
resilient in your trust
and abundant in your giving.

Know how forever you are loved,
and echo it in your self-loving.
With gratitude for your learning,
stand empowered by your choices,
cultivate your gifts,
and share your heart with the world.

Let kindness be your music,
and silence be your strength.
You are a symphony of being

and a dance of evolution.
In the heart of your intentions,
there is a jewel of creation –
your courageous human passage
from fear to love.

Be free to change the world
through your own transformation,
and, tall in your authenticity,
hang your truth among the stars.

There is only one of you
in the diversity of expressions,
weaving your precious thread
into this breathing human fabric
that we wear together as a heart
in our expanding conscious living.

CHOICE OF PEACE

Let peace be the rising breath
in this thirsty space among us,
surging from our inner nature
to become our chosen way of life.

Let kindness be the window
through which we see each other's needs,
and respect be the noble field,
where we stand by each other's truth.

Let the winds of empathy carry
deeper listening between our hearts,
and the silent stars stand witness
to the ways we grow to honor
the time and space we share together.

Let wisdom write our destiny
through each moment of awareness,
drawing clarity from our lessons,
and compassion from our mistakes.

The unwavering voice of reason,
asserted by our higher heart,

is more sensible than all
the bizarre causes for war.
The enduring vision of peace
embedded within our nature,
is more realistic than the nightmares
we so hastily accept.

This simple clarity
has long been waiting in our dreams.
Now, in our awakening,
it is the choice forever climbing
over the barbed wire fences
of our set and stubborn minds.

This choice is as transparent
as the two planets in our view –
the one where we thrive in peace,
the other where we are no more.

If we could all forgive the past,
learn from the resilience of the earth,
dwarf our agendas in her mountain,
and drown our conflicts in her lakes,
we would build bridges to a future,
where we could see each other's hearts,
and our choices would be wired to love.

DANCING IN BOTH WORLDS

On earth your soul wears a body,
as your presence in time and space,
and the vehicle for your journey
is a personality you take on.
But in worlds beyond,
where our spirit is free from time,
our presence needs not be defined,
nor can our space be confined.

We are more like timeless notes
in a weightless symphony of being,
frequencies of boundless music,
whirling as a single dancer,
as if the music were our body.
Here, we do not see self and others,
nor hear our thoughts as words.
Like waves surging from the deep,
our awareness is woven from light.

We are both individual souls
and the entire collective spirit.
We behold within our presence

every page of the human story
and each lesson of evolution.
We are both here and on earth,
as everywhere is also here,
and all times are always present,
like the unfolding of life's petals
from the flower of eternal love.

It is this love that we breathe
into your precious time on earth,
weaving it as wisdom notes
into the journey of your learning.
You are the sensitive fingers
with which we touch the earth,
the curious eyes we use
to witness your evolution.

Your passion is our heartbeat,
and your longing is our thirst.
You are us and we are you,
inseparable by time and space,
and it takes a music like life itself
to awaken this dance of grace
across the veils between the worlds.

THE TREE OF LIFE

When do we cease to see each other
as isolated nations of people,
caged by the pain of a merciless past,
and chained to a hopeless future
of un-forgiveness and distrust?

How far into the shadows
shall we cast
the illusion of otherness,
before compassion re-embraces us
back to our oneness?

The sum total of human beings
is not only humanity –
it is our call to kindness.
Our collective presence here
is not merely a world –
it is the presence of love.

May we become the early breeze
to which all hopes are born,

where we can forgive and release
what no longer serves our purpose.

There's a new tale being whispered
in the fields of our awareness,
and its stimulating fragrance
is waking hearts around the world.

The tale is of freedom,
of dignity and compassion,
and the integrity of love.
And it grows like true passion
all the way from the roots
of the eternal tree of life.

When we mature to become
this great tree of all existence,
embodying its noble spirit
in all our thoughts and our actions,
we will awake to our oneness
like a breath into life,
and like flowers on its branches
we shall forever be free.

THE SONG OF THE EARTH

If our hearts would sing
the song of this earth,
chanted with true compassion
through all of our deeds,
only silence would be heard –
the silence of deep gratitude
felt by all life upon the earth,
for our long due return to nature.

We are guardians of our future,
stewards of human hope.
Rebuilding this garden
will not be done by bricks of greed,
nor by the mortar of ambition.

It will be realized through our love,
and by our instinctive higher wisdom,
through each of our conscious choices,
fully present to the heart of life.

The vision of the earth
already lives in her song.

It flows throughout existence
with her generous abundance,
self-nurtured by her balance
and her creative zest for life.

When our love
for this precious home
will silence the rumble
of our consumption,
our emerging human song
will join the vision of the earth,
and this symphony of love
will be the gate to our rebirth.

GENERATIONAL PASSAGE

Love is ultimately stronger than fear,
and kindness will finally outlive
all the hate and exploit of this world.
It is by the call of evolution
that, in time, our human story
will migrate from the lure of power
to the interconnectedness of love.

The obsession with violence
is our historical spell,
but only a veil away
from our innate compassion.
It is through our collective choices
that the instruments of destruction
will one day be replaced
by a technology of generosity.

One of these generations
will live to see it,
but all who precede it
are part of its choosing.

To consider with humility
the footprint of our actions
on the fragile skin of tomorrow.
To expand our hearts now,
embody our humanity,
and hand over hope
to our future generations.

Evolution will accept nothing less
than the wisdom it has embedded
in the blueprints of our souls.
We may not be ready yet,
but another generation will,
and our destiny is seeded
by our present transformation.

There is not enough darkness
to block the day, however far,
in which we'll call each other
people of the heart,
and lovers of the earth,
thanking all who foresaw it,
and have chosen to never give up.

LARGER THAN FATE

You matter most,
not in your achievements,
but by whom you become
in your heart.

You blossom into love,
not into fame.
Your gifts
are sweetened by kindness,
not by the recognition
of this world.

Your true signature
is not on earth,
but in the grateful realms
of your soul,
where being is your purpose,
and sharing it is your call.

Your destiny is not a single road,
and your choices are your learning.

You are deeper than your thoughts,
and larger than fate.

In authenticity and love
is your true mastery,
and your relentless quest
is also your creation.

Each gentle breath
touching your heart
with the magic of becoming you,
is the way
you fall in love with life,
and the truest way for life itself
to live and love,
and create through you.

Epilogue

Every journey finds its deepest meaning not in its beginning nor at its ending, but in the authentic experience it inspires in the heart of the traveler. We awake on this journey, each of us in our own way and timing, in the middle of everything that's going on around us and within us. Collectively, it's like the awaking of deep magical silence in the midst of a vast sea of noise—a ripple of awareness that carries its clarity wherever it can reach.

That the world needs changing is an undeniable fact. That we are the ones on this planet who need to change, and must do so quickly, is equally clear. We know we already ride this tidal wave of change, and that it is built into our inevitable evolution, yet there is more uncertainty than assurance about its outcome. I deeply believe that in the infinite synchronicity of existence, each of us is equipped with the personal resources and individual calling to play a valuable role in this process, if we so choose. What will we choose?

Let us change our world first by whom we become, then by what we do. You are unique, and each of us is a precious link in the infinite chain of human evolution. Embrace your most authentic self, rooted in your love of life. This is when you shine the brightest. Embody the unique experience of your life's journey, and integrate your own learning to become fully present with your highest nature and gifts. Your actions will then be the music of life itself. Your choices will be the lyrics you add to it with your unique creativity and wisdom. This song of yours, and your simple presence on this planet, will not only bring value and light into the world—they will first and foremost be applauded by a standing ovation of your own heart.

To pioneer our way outside of our comfort zone, and continue learning and evolving beyond the horizons we can now see, is the essence of creativity. It is what makes this time so precious, and our collective journey as humanity so infused by hope, in spite of all the darkness that still lives in our midst. We sculpt our own being, as we ourselves are being created, transformed and refined. We paint our presence into reality, while savoring each of the present moments as catalysts for our deeper awareness.

Our capacity to change and grow so deeply from within is an understated miracle. Our ability to rewrite our stories as we read them, to exercise our magnificent free will, and edit our lives through each meaningful choice we make inside this movie—these are gifts of love and windows into the boundless compassion that embraces our existence.

Do not be intimidated by the opinions around you, or by what seems like the eternal pillars of human thinking and the unshakable structures of beliefs that dominate this world. All of it will change over time, and like palaces in the sand will return back to its un-manifested raw potential, to be reinvented as new ways of seeing and more evolved ways of living.

Find your own brilliance. At your core you are a star being, glowing from within with the intelligence of life, its relentless love, boundless imagination, and creativity. Make room in your overloaded perception of the world, for the subtle perspective of your soul.

Hear from your heart, and see through its beautiful eyes the emerging possibilities that are being freed like wild birds of hope from the harsh cages of our minds. Allow for your innate wisdom and soul gifts to bubble up to the surface of your awareness. This is your life and you can claim the space for it to blossom with your own fearless expression and inherent freedom.

In the great wall of destiny there are doors of opportunities that remain camouflaged until your intuition and maturity draw you near enough to engage them. But once they reveal themselves they are yours to open, to walk through with assertion and explore with confidence. What calls you? What tugs on your heart with the pull of love and passion? What inside you is yearning to come to life? What visions are nesting beneath the surface, waiting to take flight with your inspired choices?

I trust that this book has offered you some valuable encouragement, insight and inspiration, perhaps also some nurturing, healing, and guiding hope. It is my own passion to seek and engage with those who follow their inner whisper and step into the light of the changing times; to work with and offer my own gifts, experience and skills to those who carry a vision or a calling that requires strength, courage and clarity to bring to fruition. I write so I can share. I share so I can touch and move hearts closer to their wings. When the wings of purpose stretch wide and become airborne, there is no stopping of the grace and wonder, and no telling of the distance that hearts on purpose may cover in their flight.

Let us connect. Let us engage in this journey of evolution. Visit me on my website, and in the vast world of social media. Perhaps we'll meet in person. I offer talks, live and online, all focused on catalyzing growth, experience and purpose. I offer workshops and courses online, coaching, consulting and mentoring. And I'll be writing—a lot. I look forward to seeing what you will do, and even more what we will all become as we move closer and closer to love.

Acknowledgments

My deep gratitude to my beloved Sophia, without whom this book would still be a bird in the cage of my dreaming. Thank you for your infinite encouragement, your boundless belief in me, and all the love with which you kept pushing and vaporizing my boundaries into the stardust that turns horizons into new worlds. And for all your creative input, from the mirrors of clarity to the windows of wisdom, from the artistic touch, to the way you sounded the great bell each time an aspect of this book would reach its blossom.

Special thanks to my persistent, ever patient editor, Marilyn Jayne Owen, for her tireless, dedicated effort through all the changing texts, her eagle eye, brilliant methodical work, and heart of gold.

I am grateful to the talented Emma Grace for her exquisite artistic design of the cover and the interior, enhancing the content with her graceful eye for beauty, and her creative responsiveness to my vision for the look of the book.

I wish to thank personally each of the wonderful friends on Facebook, who persisted with their heartfelt feedback and comments, and their repeated requests to see more of my poetic expression in a book. The book is here, and it is a mirror for the way we urge each other to be all that we can be, and fully express our inner light.

And to you, the reader, I thank you for inviting my song into your space, and for being who you are, embracing your gifts, and sharing your own unique expression in this journey of evolution.

Finally, with deep gratitude to my precious family and friends, wise teachers and brilliant motivators, unexpected visitors and welcome strangers in my journey—all the faces of the biggest teacher and friend of them all—Life. I would choose no other way to grow in love.

About the Author

Yoram Weis is an insightful purpose catalyst, a soulful author, an inspiring speaker, and an experienced mentor and coach with a passion for the wisdom of the soul, the unveiling of deeper callings, and the empowering of creative visions.

On his forty-year path of learning, deep connection, and transformation, Yoram has traveled around the world extensively— initially searching and exploring, and then, as part of his work in both a senior executive role and in a mentoring capacity with a variety of international foundations and humanitarian organizations dedicated to peace education and personal development.

Over the years, he has counseled, trained, and inspired thousands of individuals from diverse nationalities, cultures, and age groups, encouraging personal growth, soul development, community awareness, and generosity in action.

Yoram currently resides with his beloved Sophia in Asheville, North Carolina, from where he coaches and consults people and organizations anywhere in the world, as the founder of Purpose Catalyst International. He is dedicated to contributing to the evolutionary shift of consciousness with his soulful, poetic writing, his inspirational talks, and his insightful workshops and mentorship.

His journey has been one of continuous transformation and evolution, discovery and creative sharing, centered around his deep commitment to his personal inner calling. His passion for continuous exploration and for the persistent integration of his experiences into his own personal growth, led him through many turns and changes, in both his personal and professional lives, arriving at his current creative work.

Yoram considers it a privilege and an honor to collaborate with and empower all who carry forth the courage of their vision in making this world a kinder and more generous place.

Please visit Yoram at **www.YoramWeis.com**
and follow him on **facebook.com/YoramJWeis**